Around the world in 30 Years

The Story of Living Hope Ministries
by Stephen Mark Brunton

ISBN: 978-1-914388-67-5

Published by Verité CM Ltd for Living Hope Ministries
Lancing, West Sussex, United Kingdom BN15 OHF
www.living-hope.org.uk
email: lhm@living-hope.org.uk

British Library Cataloguing Data
A catalogue record of this book is available from The British Library

Production management by
Verité CM Ltd, Worthing, West Sussex UK

+44 (0) 1903 241975

Printed in England

Contents

Introduction

From going on a number of missions with him myself (Poland, Ecuador, Kenya, Uganda, Rwanda and Nigeria), I can confidently and accurately declare that Richard Brunton has put himself in immensely vulnerable and challenging situations as a messenger of God on countless occasions over a number of decades. Though he did not start going into dark and dangerous places until he was 40 years old, the 40 years building up to that were vital to the work that The Lord Almighty would call him to. God-willing, he will soon reach the grand age of 75 years old and since turning 70, trips abroad have become almost completely a thing of the past. The main focus has rightly been on commissioning and supporting others to travel on his behalf instead, who have their own stories to tell.

I am not sure who will tell their stories but please read on to hear Richard's, my Dad's.

In the interests of creative writing, I have made some of the contents of this book fictional but the challenges, dangers, the main features and the countries visited are all real and true to Richard's life story. I have generally avoided using surnames of those mentioned in this book as some cannot have their surname mentioned for their safety due to persecution. For the same reason, I have also created some fictional names and intentionally avoided sharing any details that could make anyone in the book (besides a few exceptions) identifiable. Therefore, I have generally omitted information such as the names of the towns and cities Richard has visited.

The tremendous courage my Dad has shown in walking into numerous precarious and humanly speaking, insane situations, makes him my missionary hero.

Happy 75th Birthday Dad!

Mum, I cannot end this little introduction without acknowledging you! Many (including me) are in awe of how you raised five sons. Not least doing so pretty much singlehandedly at times in the early years of Living Hope Ministries whilst Dad was called overseas on mission and across the country to gain support for those missions on his own regularly. Spectacularly, this was alongside many other ways that you supported Dad and that you supported others outside of our family.

Love to you both from me and your four other sons (Paul, Phil, Matt and Jon) and our little families/tribes that naturally also stem from Richard and Elaine.

Steve/Stephen

Chapter 1

If That's What it Takes

On 28th November 1949, Richard James Sydney Brunton let out his first cries as he arrived into the world but it would not be until his teenage years that his life really began...

'Oi! Brunton!' yelled Jeremy Nesbitt.

The sound of this call was only half heard by Richard as a thick dictionary simultaneously struck the young 13 year old boy on the back of his head.

'Brunton! He's talking to you!' came another voice booming from Neville Clark.

This voice was combined with the sound of Richard's hands slapping the ground as he was tripped up, stretching out his arms to protect his face.

'What's going on here?!' came an overriding voice as Mr Topashe entered the classroom.

Not a tear fell from Richard's eyes and he refused to mention what the couple of boys had done. The brave young man literally put his head down and cracked on with his classwork and tried to forget about the incident.

After school, he walked slowly home through the fields of Fakenham, East Anglia, England and mulled over what had happened that day. It was not unusual for him to be bullied. He was quiet, very quiet and that made him vulnerable at the particular school that he attended. As he continued to ponder, he sat on a fence and watched a combine harvester driving around the fields. His attention was then taken over by a sign: 'Billy Batham Rally, Tonight at 8pm in The Market Place'.

Richard remembered that he had been invited along to this event.

He was then filled with excitement and ran the rest of the way home.

As he walked through the front door, he was greeted with these words by his mother:

'Richard! Go and wash your hands! You've got stew. It's waiting on the table. I'll give a second helping to your brother instead if you're not quick'.

Richard wolfed the stew down and began the hour long walk to 'The Market Place'. He wanted to get there as early as he could as he had been told there would be a huge attendance. Billy Batham, an American Evangelist, was a big deal.

Fakenham was booming that night which is not a usual description of the quiet Norfolk village.

As Richard entered the crowded venue, he was surprised to find the huge attendance in silence as the sole voice of Billy Batham echoed as it sprang out of the speakers. The silence was only ever broken by the odd cough and occasions of applause as Billy seemingly captivated them all. The evening ended with a time of worship as the audience sang praises to The Lord Jesus.

Richard went home that night beaming, having had an extraordinary evening.

He could not tell you exactly what Billy said that evening but he knows that whatever was said made a special penny drop in his life. As Billy spoke, God's Holy Spirit moved and Richard became sold out for Jesus: The Jesus who died and rose again about 2000 years ago to pay the price for all of humankind's sin and to offer an invitation for humankind to walk with Him every day and never be alone. This experience was no case of preaching manipulation but a genuine, true salvation.

Blown away by his Holy Spirit encounter, Richard decided that he wanted to do whatever Jesus wanted always, whatever it would take. He was clothed with a new confidence that night that was like armour and he would no longer be a quiet teenager but had been empowered that night to be a powerful preacher. No wonder that from that day on, the school bullying ceased and never returned.

Interestingly, it was not very long after this that he was informed through a prophetic message given to him in Norfolk that The Lord had a big work for him, a VERY BIG WORK!

Little did Richard know that meant he was in for a 'whole world' of adventures!

Chapter 2

To the Streets!

Not long after his conversion, Richard began to look for any opportunities that he could find to share the incomparable treasure he had found in knowing The Lord Jesus.

From Fakenham to Sculthorpe to Rainham to Rudham to wherever else he was confident The Lord was leading him, Richard preached, Bible in one hand and microphone in the other. Where there was no microphone, this young lad was not hindered as he was gifted with the lungs of an opera singer!

Though he was sometimes overwhelmed by nerves, he never allowed them to silence or stop him as he took The Gospel and the surrounding messages of that central message to the streets for any ears willing to listen and hearts ready to respond.

In these early years of preaching, Richard never heard anything clear from the recipients of the sermons he shared to know he was making an impact but that did not deter him. As Scripture affirms, there is an importance in planting seeds even if you do not get to see the fruits that they may one day produce. Richard was content to plant.

No doubt people were impacted and two onlookers were particularly impacted by God's work in and through Richard. Both of these were familiar faces...

One Saturday afternoon, near the Fakenham market stalls, as many a folk went about their business buying groceries, fresh meat, milk among other items, Richard boldly stood in the preaching square and began to speak.

'I want to tell you something this afternoon. I want to tell you some good news. I want to tell you some GREAT news!'

An elderly couple paused for a moment to listen but they were soon drawn away as the lead of their dog demanded their attention as their old husky almost pulled the man to the ground in its desire to keep walking. A young boy cycled by looking over his shoulder, smirking at Richard as he picked up that he was preaching. No-one was stopping for long to listen.

The sky began to grow grey and rain began to fall but Richard continued his sermon, not distracted by any of his surroundings, focused on his mission. About this time, a lady wearing a spotted raincoat stopped and listened. She recognised the voice of the young preacher but the rain had begun to come down heavily making it hard for her to see. It was just a short shower. As the rain stopped, the lady pulled her hood down and wiped her face with a handkerchief. As she saw Richard, she dropped her groceries on the floor. Half a dozen apples rolled down the road towards a drain. Richard stopped preaching and went to help the lady retrieve the apples. She looked at him astonished.

'Hi Mum', Richard said softly with a warm, caring smile.

She did not say a word in response. She had never seen this bold side to her son, just the quiet boy who would barely say anything and just got on with the mundane things of life, doing his homework, eating, sleeping and the occasional word of thanks to her.

That evening, unusually, Richard, his brother Michael and their parents all sat around the table ready to eat together. As usual, his mother barely had anything on her plate: just one potato, a teaspoon of peas and a small piece of chicken without gravy. The family did not have a lot and unknown to them, she was determined that her husband and sons ate as well as they could even if it meant she could not. She wanted her sons to grow up strong and healthy and her husband worked from dawn until dusk labouring, requiring much sustenance.

'So, you're a Christian now boy?!' asked his father as they all began their meals.

Richard felt unnerved by this as the tone of his father had a sarcastic twang to it.

'Yes, I am Dad' he said semi-confidently.

'Give it a week' his father said as he laughed and cut firmly into a potato.

A week passed, a month passed, years passed and Richard's faith did not depart but grew stronger and stronger and stronger.

Richard would never find out exactly what his parents made of it all in their hearts and minds but one thing was for sure: their lives were indeed impacted by his decision to follow Jesus and the transformation of Richard was a sermon in itself for them to respond to or not as they desired.

Chapter 3

Brighton

Despite his sterling behaviour and hard work, Richard failed the 11 plus and therefore, could not qualify for grammar school. He sought The Lord for wisdom on what to do. One night he particularly lifted his dilemma in prayer...

'Lord, I don't know what to do but my eyes are fixed on you' Richard gently whispered, his heart filling up with confidence as he uttered these simple but powerful words fuelled by Scripture.

In His perfect time, The Lord guided Richard to the technical college in King's Lynn and provided for him to be able to go. There he gained all the O and A-Levels that he would need for his next step.

The next step would be a bold 177 mile move down to Brighton where Richard would train to become a teacher. Though Richard felt a call from The Lord to full-time ministry, he felt that The Lord was saying that he was not ready yet and that teaching would enable an opportunity for his existing communication skills to develop further whilst gaining new attributes.

After very little opposition to his faith in Norfolk, one attribute Richard was about to have to strengthen was his ability to be true to God's Word, the Bible despite adversity.

As Richard entered the living quarters at the training college in Brighton, he was informed that he would be sharing a bedroom with two other young men around his age. Both of them were training to be Religious Studies teachers as Richard was.

The bedroom was short of space and the walls painted with a cheap magnolia colour. The room appeared to have been painted recently based on the subtle smell of paint fumes and Richard getting his bag marked as he accidentally brushed against the wall with it as he entered.

The three new roommates barely said a word to each other and not before long; they all decided it was time to hit the hay after a long day of travelling for each of them from their former homes. As he was accustomed to do before going to sleep, Richard knelt down by his bed to pray, praying silently in his head to avoid disturbing anyone.

'We will soon knock that out of you', one of the guys said mockingly.

Richard shrugged it off and continued to pray until he was content that he had prayed all that he had wanted to and then quietly got into his bed.

Chapter 4

God and a Girl

Opposition against his Bible based beliefs would continue to come as Richard journeyed towards becoming a teacher, particularly in terms of his beliefs that the world was made by The Lord and in six days, along with other fundamentalist beliefs that were ridiculed by many. He was seen as childish to believe that the events of the Bible were historical accounts rather than metaphorical but Richard believed that to not view the events this way was to have a lack of faith in The Lord's power, ability and sovereignty. Furthermore, he felt it would put humankind in the driving seat of each life rather than The Lord to pick and choose what was and was not to be taken literally and would easily turn the Bible into just another book rather than revering it as God's Word.

Richard was not alone in his thinking and he found great joy in being around like-minded people at the Christian Union on campus that he in time would go on to lead. He did not need anyone to affirm his thinking. He was headstrong in his beliefs but it was nice to not be alone.

One evening as he carried his Bible shamelessly across campus to the chapel for the Christian Union weekly meeting, he heard someone playing the piano as he approached the chapel's main entrance. He quietly opened the doors and took a seat and listened.

A young lady with long, black hair elegantly and gracefully danced on the keys with her fingers as she worshipped The Lord through the instrument.

Richard applauded as she finished and the young lady, Elaine blushed and commented on mistakes that she had made.

Elaine would become Richard's highlight of attending Christian Union and he increasingly found good excuses to spend as much time with her as possible. United by their devotion to The Lord and attracted to one another with their very different but unique bright qualities, they took that well-known journey from friends to 'just friends' to courting.

Little did they know that they would not before long exchange rings and go on to celebrate their Golden Wedding Anniversary in 2023!

Chapter 5

Juggling

Back we go to the '70s after that glimpse into the future and Richard's next significant challenge would be learning to juggle!

After graduating as a teacher and beginning a full-time post in that occupation, Richard took on the voluntary role of pastor at West Hoathly Evangelical Church in 1974.

By this time in his life, Richard was highly experienced in preaching but the main lesson of West Hoathly would be learning to deliver pastoral care. Although the size of the congregation only ranged on average between 12-20 people, there were many people in the community who expected Richard's services. They saw the West Hoathly chapel as theirs and would lean on him in times of difficulty and sadness, especially in the event of losing loved ones.

Facing the impact of the darkness of death and serious illnesses would be a frequent occurrence in these times. Richard understandably struggled in the early days of these new challenges.

On one occasion, he visited a lady to offer comfort and solace after she had sadly experienced a stroke and Richard came out of the visit looking more unwell than the lady!

However, Richard learnt to handle difficult situations well and thankfully his time pastoring West Hoathly was not all doom and gloom. Many were baptised in Jesus' name in Richard's time serving as pastor and Richard would indeed act as a torch to help guide many out of the tunnels they found themselves in.

Being a full-time teacher and feeling like a full-time pastor would prepare Richard well for supporting pastors in the future, some of whom would have even more commitments than Richard and many pastors ever would.

The skill of juggling would have to increase further when Richard and Elaine had their five children: Paul, Philip, Matthew, Stephen and Jonathan.

Stephen and Jonathan would be born in the Clarendon days in Hove which would be Richard and Elaine's next chapter!

Chapter 6

Clarendon's Calling

The then, family of five (Richard, Elaine, Paul, Philip and Matthew) had a call from The Lord to move from West Hoathly to a church in Hove called Clarendon (now known as 'Emmanuel'). The first sparks of the call came through a conversation between Richard and a man called Terry whilst the family of five were still in West Hoathly. The Lord used a comment that Terry made to trigger a sense in Richard that he and the family needed to take a leap of faith. He and Terry did not realise that this would in fact mean joining the church Terry led but Richard knew that it would mean leaving West Hoathly behind. Richard had grown attached to the people and they to him so this was no easy move but with that peace beyond understanding that only The Lord can give, Richard and the family took the leap!

Whilst continuing to teach as his paid occupation, Richard soon became an elder without the title at Clarendon and in time, was given the huge responsibility of overseeing four of the Clarendon church house groups. These were groups where between half a dozen and a dozen attenders of the church would gather to worship, talk about Scripture and pray for one another about different challenges they were facing, very much like how many house groups run today. One of these house groups was in Hollingbury, another in Patcham, the third in Westdean and finally, a new plant where they lived in Coldean which Richard and Elaine pioneered.

The numerous and intense issues that arise from overseeing one house group can be quite a feat so to oversee four was a great challenge to prepare Richard for his next step and for an international ministry which at this stage he had no idea was in God's BIG plan for him.

The next step for the (by the end of the Clarendon days), family of SEVEN would be another new calling and another significant move and an exciting opportunity for Richard to become a full-time minister like he had always desired. This would be a paid occupation allowing him to leave his teaching career, leading a church plant in a village called Lancing.

One tremendous blessing that The Lord gave Richard and the family in response to their leap of faith to move to Clarendon was providing a mortgage for them in a spectacular way!

A wonderful, wholehearted Christian lady shared the cost of a mortgage with them and after living with them for a short time, moved on whilst leaving them with her share of the finances and therefore her share of the home!

Not only did this bless the family tremendously in the Clarendon days but it gave them the ability to purchase another mortgage in Lancing where The Lord moved powerfully again. The Lord ensured that the price was exactly what Richard and Elaine could match when the housing agent in Lancing overruled the previous mortgage owner who requested more than they could have afforded.

Chapter 7

Church Politics

Before The Lord miraculously provided a mortgage in Lancing in 1991, Richard and his family continued to live in Coldean when Richard first became pastor of the Clarendon church plant in Lancing in 1990. The plant was called Grace church and is now known as 'The Redeemer Church' and has been situated in a town called Worthing rather than in Lancing for quite some time now.

Richard's time pastoring there was sadly not a very happy one for him or the family. It got off to a tough start when Richard realised that many of the members of his initial congregation who had also previously been at the Clarendon mother church in Hove had their hearts set on someone else being the first pastor. Their surprise and disappointment that their choice of pastor was not selected, meant Richard had a congregation that were not behind him in the same way as he and any pastor would hope for.

Thankfully there were some 'keen supporters' of Richard who had moved over from the mother church in the congregation, ensuring Richard was not too downhearted and was one form of affirmation for him that he was God's choice for the role even if he was not the majority of the church's.

However, as time went on the majority heaped on pressure, making it clear that the ideas they had for how the church should be led were not the same as how Richard was leading it. Richard never did anything untoward and never made any unusual mistakes for a pastor but he was simply fighting a losing battle. He was trying to win over a majority that were never going to truly accept his way of leading when they had another way of leading so fixed in their minds even before he had been appointed.

Grace church was Clarendon's first church plant and was a steep learning curve for everybody.

Unfortunately, Richard and his family were the main casualties of all of the rising tensions within the church politics. In the end, Richard was informed by a distant overseer of the church that he needed to step down. Richard was encouraged to go back to teaching and he and the family naturally had to leave the church without a church home to go to as one of the major consequences of this.

It was May 1994 and one thought that left Richard feeling bewildered was that four days before he was made redundant, a dear brother in Christ had given him a special word at a prayer meeting that Richard had attended.

The word was: *'God is going to open up your ministry and it will open up and develop. You should be sure of your call Richard'.*

Richard wondered what on earth was going on. His ministry was closing not opening!

However, it was not what was occurring on earth that mattered. Something was stirring in heaven!

Chapter 8

One Name and One Number!

As Richard sought The Lord's direction, he felt the beginnings of a call! Though he had never been to Kenya before, he sensed that he should go there. This was partly through a word from his friend Simon of Freedom Embassy Ministries International and partly a direct leading from The Lord.

Richard and the family were naturally in trouble financially after the unexpected and sudden redundancy and the money they did have had to rightly be prioritised for looking after the whole family's basic needs.

So Richard made it simple...

'Lord, if you want me to go to Kenya, I want to go but I know you would not want me to go at the detriment of my family. They have been through enough already. Please provide the money for me to go to Kenya outside of the finances I already have as a clear sign that You want me to go'.

Sure enough, The Lord provided and wonderfully. One of the contributions was particularly special where a friend gave £100 that they themselves did not even have. They prayed for finances to help Richard and as they did so, their letterbox rattled and there was the cash! The God of the Acts of the Apostles is the same God today doing the same kind of things even in this world increasingly full of doubt, hypocrisy and blasphemy.

Now the finances had been provided, the flights were soon booked and Richard was scheduled to join his friend Simon himself for a mysterious trip to Kenya. The trip then became even more mysterious when Simon had to pull out! Simon's wife delivered the news to Richard at the airport just before they were due to fly after a delayed first attempt.

'I am so sorry Richard. For complicated reasons Simon cannot go but there's nothing to stop you Richard!'

She then placed a piece of paper in his hand and spoke again, delivering an unsettling yet thrilling instruction that she believed was from The Lord.

'You must go'.

As she walked away, Richard opened the piece of paper which revealed the name of a pastor and his telephone number.

Anxiety and confusion whispered cruelly in Richard's head but then he felt a voice of truth and reason speak powerfully over them. He was reminded by The Lord that it was He who had called him to go and He would go with him. Simon may have invited him but it was The Lord who had called Richard to this trip and adventure.

'Well, Lord, it's over to you' Richard said respectfully as he shook off the anxiety and confusion and headed towards the departure gate.

Chapter 9

Kenya

When Richard arrived in Nairobi, he was greeted with the kind of air that wraps around you like an unwanted thick coat on a summer's day and the strange sight of orange soil. He waited and waited, with the one number he had been given not answering as he rang repeatedly. He waited for over an hour for the one name he had been given prior to the flight to arrive: Edward Tambo. The temptation to panic was breathing down Richard's neck but naturally added extra heat rather than any relief. Eventually, an old vehicle that looked kind of like a retro Peugeot rocked up accompanied by a friendly, smiling face. Edward had arrived!

Thankfully, though Edward was the only contact Richard had prior to the flight, he was not the only contact Richard had been given since the flight making Richard sweat less when he reached Nairobi...

Being a curious fellow, not long after boarding the plane, Richard asked if he could see the flight deck as you were allowed to back then and his request was quickly accepted. The stewardess arranged this exciting opportunity and took his name to ensure he was not forgotten. Richard decided to call himself 'Pastor Richard Brunton'. After all, he had lost his job, not his title and not his calling. Little did Richard know that the choice to still refer to himself in this way would lead to a far more exciting opportunity than a flight deck!

Picking up on his title, toward the end of the flight, the stewardess invited Richard to speak at her church and gave him a second name and a second number that he could refer to when he landed. This one was for Bishop Arthur Gatonga.

Bishop Arthur would provide a mammoth amount of opportunities for Richard to begin to fulfil his strengthened calling including speaking to a congregation in a 6,000 seater tent and leading a prayer time entitled 'Morning Glory' every day at a conference centre. It was wonderful for Richard to be able to reach as many people as possible to help them grow in their walks with The Lord and he even saw people healed and converted during the trip as God moved mightily through him and around him.

Part of Richard missed the comfortable norms of jolly England but his soul was touched by The Lord and on fire, leading him forward and above the desires of earthly comforts.

As he saw The Lord moving, he felt like he was home spiritually and whether he spoke to one person in a mud hut or a mass gathering, his heart was full of joy and humility as he simply gave his all in each situation, first and foremost for The Lord.

As this first adventure drew to an end, Richard felt strongly that he would not be returning to any Clarendon related church or seeking a church in England to pastor. The Only God, our Holy Triune God was speaking with a megaphone that He was doing a new thing and therefore the old were things of the past not the future.

God is GREAT and GOOD and He ensured that Richard was blessed for his major step of faith in catching a flight to deep, dark Africa on his own. The connection with Edward proved to be a significant blessing but equally, if not more so was the connection made on the plane to Nairobi itself. In fact, you could say that perhaps the one name and one number were in a way primarily God's method of choice to get Richard on the plane, to give him new wings and once on the flight, God's plans along with Richard started to soar as Living Hope Ministries was beginning to take off!

Chapter 10

Uganda

Living Hope Ministries was essentially born out of that first trip. The redundant congregational pastor, Richard Brunton was never made redundant by God and was increasingly going to be a pastor for pastors! He would train pastors and support pastors with responsibility for far more than what man had taken away from him.

The title for the ministry arose from Richard and Elaine coming across the following Scripture during their journey of discerning an appropriate title…

'Praise be to the God and Father of our Lord Jesus Christ! In his great mercy he has given us new life into a <u>living hope</u> through the resurrection of Jesus from the dead'

1 Peter 1: 3

'Living Hope' would be the perfect title for the ministry as Richard desired a title that would put the focus totally on Jesus rather than on himself at all. Furthermore, this title would summarise the aim of the work well: The Lord was giving 'Living Hope' to Richard, Elaine and the family after a season of darkness and rejection from the world and Richard would take the message of Jesus, The Living Hope to many!

A very dear friend called Ray would advise Richard that it should be 'Ministries' rather than 'Ministry' as the work would be so broad. After officially becoming a charity in 1995, the work continued to expand with that initial mission proving to be even more significant than Richard had realised.

The 'Morning Glory' prayer times that Richard had led on his first trip to Kenya were not only the dawn of Richard's Kenyan adventures rising but in time, they would prove to be God's miraculous way of giving Richard the keys to other countries in Africa. Uganda would be one of those countries...

The event organiser of the 'Morning Glory' prayer times connected Richard to a gentleman from Uganda called Moses. After getting to know Moses to a strong enough extent that Richard felt another call from God had begun, he ventured to see Moses in Uganda in 1997.

The Lord graciously once again blessed and protected Richard as he travelled to numerous settings ranging from large conferences to small slum gatherings and the friendship with Moses was a blessing.

As the work in Uganda developed, Richard and Moses pondered the future. It seemed clear to both of them that the plans they each had contained contrasts that would make it inevitable for them to part company at some point but with no ill feeling either side.

A man named Peter began attending a number of the conferences in Uganda where Richard was preaching. Through this, Richard and Peter began conversations that would lead to this new friend eventually becoming Richard's main long-term contact for Uganda.

Peter, his wife Rose and their children along with the school and choir they oversee, would become dear friends and connections for Richard, his family and many others in the United Kingdom.

A child sponsorship program and UK visits from Peter and his family and their choir made it easy for these friendships and connections to come into fruition.

A particularly distinct and unique memory of Uganda for Richard and many other Living Hope Ministries' missioners has been baptising hundreds in Lake Victoria over the years. The possibility of crocodiles in the water makes it appropriate that the baptisms are held with respect and reverence but are short rather than snappy!

Chapter 11

Tanzania

The Morning Glory prayer times that Richard led on his first trip to Kenya also opened up a door to Tanzania. Richard met a man named Stephen at the conference connected with the prayer times. Stephen, who would later become known as Bishop Stephen, would prove to be one of Richard's greatest friends on his Living Hope Ministries' adventures and in life generally.

Although Stephen lived in Kenya, one of his main focuses was Tanzania and Richard accompanied him to countless churches in Tanzania that Stephen was connected with due to his role as founder of 'Great Commission churches of Tanzania'.

The first trip took place in 1998 with many more to follow.

The mighty mountain of Kilimanjaro is a spectacular feature of the country and Richard has many memories of the Golden Rose Hotel in Arusha where he spent many a night on his travels. It always put a smile on Richard's face to find a Gideon Bible in whichever room of the hotel he would stay. They acted as an encouraging reminder that he was not the first English speaking missioner to go there and that he like others was building upon the Kingdom work that others had begun long ago.

The border crossing to Tanzania was often a memorable experience. The security was particularly vigorous, making it not feel like such a warm welcome for Richard each time despite the weather being of a high temperature as usual.

Stephen and Richard instantly had a deep connection. Their transparency, boldness for Jesus and vision for church planting in a humble manner with a pastoral care emphasis made for quite the brotherhood.

Driving along with Stephen in cars that were probably passed their sell by date on rocky roads, laughing and joking whilst talking about serious matters at other times are some of the most wonderful memories.

Sadly for us but happy for him, Stephen went to be with The Lord in 2014 and a gentleman called William now oversees the Living Hope Ministries work in Tanzania.

Like with any man or woman who truly lives for The Lord Jesus, Stephen's legacy lives on despite death and no power of hell can stop it! Not now, not ever! The Lord may change its direction and shape as times change but Kingdom work is often unseen as it is not of this world, though in this world so can only ever grow!

Chapter 12

Rwanda

Whilst preaching in a slum area in Uganda, Richard looked discerningly at the humble congregation gathered before him as he sought to serve them in every way God might be leading him to. They eagerly listened to him as he preached from the Bible, hanging on every single word. In a typical layout for this kind of situation, the elderly and vulnerable sat upon basic plastic chairs in a mud hut as the others sat on the dirt or stood. They all enjoyed shelter together from the blazing sun.

Richard searched their faces as he spoke, prayerfully trying to decide who he could pass on the limited number of Bible commentaries he had with him that he planned to hand out to those that could make best use of them. Some lived locally and were known to Richard's co-leaders but others had travelled many miles to be there, eager to hear from this Englishman that had grown quite famous among the poor.

One face particularly stood out to Richard. There was a man with a particularly warm smile who seemed to grasp the sermon Richard was preaching more than his peers. He nodded in a manner of agreement rather than solely appreciation. After the sermon, the man approached Richard…

'Thank you brother Richard. That was most encouraging and informative' he said.

After nodding and shaking his hand in response, Richard then lent down, unzipped his bag and placed one of the Bible commentaries into his hands.

'This is a gift for you if you can use it to teach others?'

The man held the Bible to his heart and looked up exclaiming: *'Thank You Lord for this gift for Rwanda!'*

Upon hearing these words, Richard was amazed. This gentleman had travelled all the way from Rwanda to be at the conference. That was quite some journey! In addition to that, Richard's amazement simultaneously stemmed from seeing how The Lord was using Living Hope Ministries to reach people in other countries without him having to even enter those countries! As Living Hope Ministries would continue to develop in the future, Richard and others would see more and more of this in different ways. The Lord has multiple plans beneath the plans we see and work towards.

Due to the horrific genocide that had taken place in Rwanda in 1994, Richard had always hoped that he could be of some help to the Rwandans so it was highly pleasing to him to see that begin to come into fruition.

The Rwandan that Richard had met that day, turned out to be a Bishop called Augustine who had planted churches in both Uganda and Rwanda. He had experienced the genocide to the point that there were bullet holes in the walls of his home church! Due to the genocide, he had lived in Uganda for a season with his family when they had literally run for their lives for refuge. This is how he had strong connections in Uganda and how he had ended up at the gathering where he received a Bible commentary that would indeed be a blessing for Rwanda. It would even be a blessing beyond Rwanda as quite similarly to Richard, Augustine would travel to various places to teach the Word of God.

Richard and Augustine developed a special and strong friendship leading to Rwanda becoming one of the countries that Richard would most frequently visit to preach, teach and offer pastoral support.

One unique message that The Lord would give Richard to share in Rwanda over the years would be particularly significant and have an important impact.

In just one month during the genocide, nearly a million people lost their lives in Rwanda demonstrating its devastating impact. In light of this fact and guidance through The Holy Spirit, Richard felt strongly to deliver the following message...

'The Lord will save as many as were lost in the genocide!' Richard boldly proclaimed.

It would be impossible to prove that this will or would become true but one thing is for sure, it does appear to be the case that revival usually comes after severe tragedy affirming that the above words were indeed words from above.

Chapter 13

Poland

As the links in Africa continued to develop, The Lord revealed that He had more than one continent in mind for Richard to serve. The next continent would technically be his home continent but not a part of it that had much in common with the UK.

Back in the days when the world had not yet entered the 21st Century, The Lord spoke to Richard through an African friend called Sam...

'Brother Richard, The Lord has shown me something that I must share with you' Sam said.

'Thank you brother. Please do tell me', Richard replied.

'The Lord has told me that He is going to open a door in Eastern Europe for you. You must go through it and continue in your calling'.

A few days after this prophetic message, Richard was handed some papers from a lady called Chris who belonged to a church in Suffolk. Suffolk is not too far away from where Richard was born and grew up but it was galaxies apart in terms of football team allegiance!

However, the papers were nothing to do with the 'Old Farm Derby' football frenzy. They contained information on Chris' work: 'European Partners in Christ'. This is also known as EPIC! The information that the papers contained proved to be affirmation of a call to Eastern Europe and Richard began to prayerfully ponder how to begin this next venture.

Chris and Richard discussed different options and The Lord appeared to shine a light on Poland as Richard's starting point for taking Living Hope Ministries' fellowship and Bible teaching to Eastern Europe.

Andrzej, the President of the Evangelical Alliance in Poland would be Richard's first and also continuous key contact in Poland. As Richard travelled out for his first trip there in 1999, he embraced a friendship that would lead him to preach all across that country. Andrzej and another gentleman called Julian would drive Richard to numerous preaching venues including Warsaw which even to this day bears scars of the holocaust that took place during World War 2.

Guided and equipped by The Holy Spirit, Richard would do his best then and for many years to come to be a voice and presence of God's healing for the people of Poland.

Chapter 14

Bosnia

It took less than a year for Richard to see The Lord Almighty's work through him in Eastern Europe go beyond Poland as specified in the prophecy's finer details. Chris would once again be the key that The Lord would choose to unlock an Eastern European country as she connected Richard with a church in Bosnia.

After a complicated start with leadership and pastoral issues within that initial church that were beyond Richard's capability of solving, a man named Zeljko became Richard's Bosnian co-worker through The Lord graciously bringing good out of the church mess.

Zeljko had been a casualty of what were cruel and corrupt pastoral behaviours in the church just described but The Lord saw his suffering and his heart to do His will and lifted him out of the ashes, appointing him to work with Richard as Living Hope Ministries' Bosnia representative as expressed and to also lead a church!

Broken people flocked to Zeljko like as the Bible puts it 'Sheep without a shepherd', asking him to lead them and with God's affirmation and God's help, he did, has and does.

Like a number of the pastors Richard works with, Zeljko initially and even to a degree long-term, carried on with his paid work outside of the church whilst investing most of the rest of his time to the church. He is a trained psychologist and continued to teach in that field regularly to provide for his family and himself and to avoid putting a financial weight on the church in its infancy.

Richard has been a great support to Zeljko over the years and Zeljko has been a great encouragement to Richard.

One key moment in their friendship was when Richard felt that The

Lord was leading him to phone Zeljko to deliver a simple but highly important message...

'Hello Zeljko, are you free to talk?'

'Hello Richard, yes absolutely' Zeljko replied quickly and warmly.

'Zeljko, I really sense that The Lord wants me to tell you to keep going and to not give up'.

Little did Richard know that at that exact time Zeljko was feeling so battered and bruised spiritually that he had started to consider leaving the church he had begun leading. He was tempted to head back to his birthplace, Croatia where he would have had an easier time and a better standard of living for himself and his family.

After deep prayer and reflection, Zeljko decided to remain in Bosnia and to graciously focus on what was unseen rather than what is temporary as he soon realised he was where The Lord wanted him to be. The call from Richard was one of the significant affirmations that Zeljko had received to help him persevere.

As time has gone on, Zeljko has planted two churches from the church that he leads. This particularly demonstrates how The Lord has blessed Zeljko and the work that He has called him to do and how suffering does not have to be the end of a story.

Sometimes, it seems that the sun sets before it rises and Zeljko has increasingly seen that it was certainly worth staying in Bosnia!

Chapter 15

Romania

In a new millennium, through his link with Chris, Richard embarked on his first Romanian adventure! A pastor called John would be Richard's key contact there and John would open up some very different doors to those opened by Andrzej in Poland. Unlike Poland, most of the doors that would open would be to people's homes rather than church buildings.

Due to poverty and other challenges facing the churches that John was connected to, many of the churches would meet in their homes rather than in a building set apart for public worship to The Lord and public teaching of His Word, the Bible.

Reverence and respect are still present in the services despite being in homes and one family particularly ensure that by setting one room in their homes apart to specifically and solely be used for worship and teaching. Richard has even experienced and participated in communion, baptism and dedication services in some of the Romanian homes over the years and has played a part in ensuring these priceless acts of devotion have been Biblically sound.

Inevitably, due to the size and layouts of homes when compared with church buildings, far fewer people attended the various services Richard has attended and served at in comparison to some of the gigantic gatherings of other trips, particularly Africa.

However, this did not take away from the quality and the worth of those visits and just like African and other brothers and sisters Richard had met and would meet on his Living Hope Ministries' adventures, the Romanians would show a wealth greater than gold in their love and passion for The Lord Jesus, making each trip a heavenly lesson and an inspiration. One event particularly illustrates that...

'John, what are we doing here?' Richard politely asked as John pulled up after a short car journey following their very un-English but kind breakfast of bread and ham that Richard had stuck his teeth into at a small café in Transylvania.

'To baptise brother' John replied.

'Excellent. Where will we baptise?' Richard asked as he looked around seeing no sign of a swimming pool, beach, lake or even a pond.

John pointed to a nearby object that looked like a small skip for rubbish. Richard then saw a man walking back and forth from his home, carrying huge buckets of water, one in each hand to fill up the skip.

A small group then began to sing songs of worship unaccompanied by any instrument. Richard was then invited to speak on the meaning of baptism and a young man named Alexandru stepped forward to be baptised in the skip. He did not care that it was a very humble ceremony in every way. It mirrored something of the humility of The Lord Jesus Christ who chose 33 years of poverty and hardship on earth when He could have lived a life of luxury.

Like Alexandru, many of the Christians of Romania resemble something of the manger lifestyle Jesus chose and that these Romanians were and are not overcome by.

Their eyes are fixed on the things of heaven, things eternal not temporary, albeit not constantly but enough to ensure their hearts pound with worship to our Holy Triune God in their songs and lives!

Chapter 16

Nigeria

Over the years, Living Hope Ministries has increasingly had a television and radio presence in addition to its other areas of service. Both have been invaluable but the story of how the television work emerged is perhaps more unusual. It all started when a lady from an influential broadcasting station called 'Lighthouse Television' in Uganda attended a seminar where Richard was speaking in a Ugandan slum. She had been invited by Richard's long-term contact and friend in Uganda, Peter. She was so impacted by the anointing that she could see The Lord had graciously poured out on Richard that she was keen for him to start making television programs for Lighthouse Television to air.

Sure enough, Living Hope Ministries' teachings would feature on Lighthouse Television and in time, they would also be aired elsewhere and through other avenues...

In 2001, whilst visiting one of the churches in Southern England that supported the ministry, Richard was approached by a Nigerian gentleman keen to speak to him about an idea that he had.

'Richard, I have a good friend in Nigeria called Bitrus. He is a Bishop and has great connections with a broadcasting station. I think that he would be keen to put some of your programs on their channel. What do you think?'

Richard and Elaine prayed on this suggestion. As usual, they did not want to make any big decisions without seeking The Lord first. As they prayed, Richard felt he should get in touch with Bishop Bitrus directly and it seemed clear that it would be right to see Bitrus and Nigeria.

This would indeed lead to television programmes being aired from and in Nigeria but the adventures to Nigeria would be equally, if not even more so, significant.

It was not a light decision to go to Nigeria as it was and is one of the most notorious countries in Africa due to its dangers including great hostility between Muslims and Christians.

It is true to say that not all Muslims are violent and that many are in fact peace-loving and treat others with care and it is also true to say that sadly some Christians in Nigeria and elsewhere are equally to blame for causing horrific and unspeakable harm.

Thankfully, Bishop Bitrus and those he worked with closely were clearly peacemakers so Richard was delighted to meet them and able to sincerely trust them with his life in dangerous circumstances. Unfortunately, the Muslims nearby were not friendly folk.

Very careful and thorough planning would be needed for all of Richard's visits to ensure his and others' safety. The pressures and challenges were varied and vast. Being so close to the equator meant fairly extreme heats and a climate of large lizards being as present as pigeons in Trafalgar Square. Such things would be the last thing on Richard's mind however as he kept his attention and focus on seeking The Lord for the right word for each situation and then delivering it. More of a concern to him was the hostility of the particular groups of Muslim extremists nearby. Meetings were at times cancelled at the last minute due to very real threats and on one occasion the opposition was so close that the room next door to Richard's was raided. It appeared they targeted the wrong room by God's grace and no-one was harmed. The presence of witchcraft is strong in Africa and especially in particular countries including Nigeria. Witchcraft is no subject for ridicule as the following Nigerian story demonstrates and it is only one example of countless others...

Deep in a slum, a man dressed in a purple one-piece garment walked threateningly past the villagers. To avoid eye contact with the man, those who passed him, kept their eyes on the ground, terrified of him and the power Satan had given him. Entrapped by Satan themselves, they had no belief for his or their own deliverance. As some villagers watched secretly from a distance, they witnessed the man enter his home and leave it without a door. Through sorcery, the man would be heard moving around in the home and then suddenly appear out of nowhere meditating on his knees outside of the home. There were no smoke and mirrors. This was Satan at work similar to how we hear of Egyptians turning their staffs into snakes and water into blood in Exodus 7. However, we also hear in Exodus 7 of Aaron, a follower of The One True God having his staff turned into a snake by God and that staff swallows the Egyptians' staffs!

We need to be careful to not be tricked into following Satan with his impressive but evil sorcery and to follow The Lord Almighty who unlike Satan performs spectacular feats that lead to no harm on those He works through.

It appeared that the sorcerer near Minna had no interest in being set free from Satan but a lady in the village approached a female missioner called Sandra who accompanied Richard and the rest of the team on that trip.

'I have headaches!' the lady yelled.

'Dark headaches all the time' she sobbed.

Sandra looked and saw strange-looking black wristbands on her arms.

'What are they for?' Sandra gently asked.

'Witchcraft. Please help me' she begged.

'I am afraid I cannot help you but I know someone who can' Sandra said.

'Please' the lady replied whimpering the word out in desperation. Sandra paused and prayed in her head, seeking God's guidance.

'Take off the wrist bands and I believe The Lord Jesus will set you free'.

The lady fearfully took off the wrist bands.

'They're gone' declared the lady faintly, exhausted from the relentless inner attack she had been facing constantly for what felt like her whole life. Free at last, her face looked different; it looked peaceful, healthier. The headaches and the demons that caused them had left her because of The Lord Jesus.

Chapter 17

Northern Ireland

Richard has had the privilege of explicitly serving The Lord in some way in every country within the UK and also its close neighbours, the Republic of Ireland. Out of these countries, besides England where he has countless memories due to living there, it is his time in Northern Ireland that is most memorable.

Back in 1992, Richard felt led to take a team from England to Northern Ireland to encourage a friend of a friend who pastored a church in Coleraine. Northern Ireland was suffering greatly due to what would historically be known as 'The Troubles' where there was much bloodshed and even death as Catholics and Protestants fought one another for complex reasons. The Lord put a team together and they flew to Northern Ireland's capital, Belfast to then travel to Coleraine in order to pray with and support Pastor Maurice and others.

The above trip happened to be Richard's first flight anywhere and a decade later he returned but this time alone. Through phone calls and emails, Richard developed and retained a solid friendship with Maurice and Maurice was keen to support Living Hope Ministries where he could and gratefully continued to receive pastoral support from Richard himself.

The Troubles had left and would leave an aftermath that would lead Richard, Elaine and others to keep the people of Northern Ireland in their prayers. Many prayers for The Lord to send help to the country would be poured out and would continue to be poured out. Little did Richard and Elaine realise that their son Steve and their daughter-in-law Charlene would play a part in one of the answers to that prayer.

Since his first visit to Northern Ireland in 2006, Steve had a heavy heart for the country and the city of Belfast. In time, that heavy heart would develop into a call to move over there and to be a part of the community and a part of the healing and 'Good News' sharing needed.

The key word that The Lord gave Steve for himself and his little family would be that The Lord Himself would do *'the extraordinary in the ordinary'*.

Charlene, who was born in Belfast felt ready for a return after Steve sensed the calling and accompanied by their two children (one still in the womb), they made the big move to Belfast in 2021. The sense of calling was so strong that they booked the tickets before Steve had acquired a job and before acquiring a long-term home. The whole story of that adventure is a story for another time but one significant part of the story has been Steve handing out tracts on his own on the famous Shankill Road or as he calls it: 'Holding out Hope'. In recent times, The Lord has called others to serve with Steve so he now has the privilege of leading and training an outreach team.

Chapter 18

Malawi

In 2004, a good friend called Mark, who pastored a church in Worthing near to where Richard and Elaine lived, invited Richard to join him on a mission to Malawi. Mark had a strong connection there and had visited there previously. With both Richard and Mark having a big heart for Africa and a good friendship with one another, it seemed a godly idea to take a trip there together.

Richard quickly connected well with the Malawian people. Although there were some clear cultural differences to other African countries he had visited, it was still Africa so Richard was very used to the patterns, behaviours and mannerisms that are present throughout the whole continent. Having many areas of extreme poverty is of course one deeply sad familiarity that each country shares.

Unlike in some of the other African countries, Richard detected a strong sense of ritualistic Christianity in Malawi that remains to this day. There were and are a great number of Malawians that believe they are Christians but actually just follow ritualistic behaviours that they have labelled as Christian or are of Christian origin but have been distorted. They like others in the world, including some in the UK, are bound up in fear, anger and hurt by biblical and non-biblical rules and regulations rather than being true children of God who follow biblical rules and regulations out of love.

In Malawi, it is particularly common for church leaders to attend conferences who do not actually know and follow The Lord Jesus themselves. In some cases, if not many cases, this is done so unknowingly. They think that they know Jesus because they know the Ten Commandments and other biblical commands but they do not know the heart behind them or The Holy Spirit behind them! It has been wonderful and astounding for Richard and others to see many leaders become born again at these conferences. Through these conferences and other means, God has helped them to find a true relationship with Him where they live for Him as Lord following biblical commands correctly rather than intentionally or not, the commandments being their god instead. The beautiful domino effect of this is that the congregations of these leaders can then be shown The Way, The Truth and The Life through their converted leaders! This is one cause of revival in the world as leaders naturally impact many lives.

Malawi became another country that Living Hope Ministries would serve and as time went on, Richard gained a consistent contact in Malawi called Aubrey who remains the consistent contact to this day. However, on this occasion, it would not be Richard who would initiate this African contact originally but other representatives of Living Hope Ministries.

Two of Richard and Elaine's longest and closest friends, Dave and Claire, who moved from the UK to New Zealand in 2002 (another great God story!) teamed up with Bishop Stephen from Kenya to visit Malawi a few years after Richard's initial trip there.

At a conference, all three felt drawn to Aubrey with Claire particularly sensing this was another divine appointment for Living Hope Ministries. Sure enough it was and among other things, Aubrey would become the master of the Mobile Phone Conferences, utilising the option of them regularly to ensure those he serves receive sound teaching of the Word. The Mobile Phone Conferences are an integral part of Living Hope Ministries' work that I will refer to again in a little more detail in the final chapter of this book.

Chapter 19

Pakistan

The Living Hope Ministries' website and social media have been priceless assets, enabling people to discover the charity from anywhere and everywhere.

Through the website, Richard received this email towards the end of 2004...

'Dear brother, I am very happy to hear of the work of Living Hope Ministries. My name is Rasheed from Pakistan. I wonder would you like to fellowship?'

As Richard found this message in his junk mail, he pondered what to do. If he replied, would his computer or emails get hacked? Was this man going to be yet another individual asking for lots of money that Richard did not have?

Richard prayerfully replied and rather than experiencing any IT or other issues, he began to experience some great conversations over email with Rasheed. The two brothers in Christ formed a friendship through this way.

Although the signal was not always strong, they then strengthened the friendship through praying over the telephone. This was when Richard felt they really got to know one another. He thought to himself: 'You can hear a person's words when they are talking but you hear their heart when they are praying'. Once again, Richard had been introduced to another brother with a similar heart to him through God's wonderful sovereign ways.

All of this combined was enough for Richard to feel confident that a trip to Pakistan would be a good next step despite the dangers of Pakistan. It is worth noting that the hostility in Pakistan was and is even sharper than the hostility of Nigeria and other particularly challenging parts of Africa. For that reason, Richard would be in need of weightier protection than he had received in Africa.

After a long flight and complicated VISA process where Richard had to be particularly vigilant in describing himself as a teacher rather than missioner for his protection, Richard's feet (and thankfully, whole body) entered Rasheed's home safe and sound. He was delighted to meet Rasheed and his wife Aiza but surprised to also meet a man holding a rifle...

'It's ok Richard' Rasheed said seeing Richard's eyes nervously looking at the rifle.

'He's here to look after you'.

Sure enough, that was the man's purpose with him even lying low on the roof of the home overnight, watching out for any intruders who may have seen the white man, presumed to be wealthy, enter it.

The extreme poverty and extreme persecution of Christians in Pakistan means that the spiritual temperature is very high. Those who are bold for Jesus there and elsewhere in such conditions experience the sometimes literal and often spiritual bullets that come with being such a frontline Christian. However, they also experience a front row seat for miracles and supernatural wonders. The Lord blesses the boldness and faith of those who step out for Him as He leads them and empowers them and this is perhaps why Richard and others have seen many more miracles and supernatural healings in countries like Pakistan than they have in the UK.

The first trip to Pakistan took place in 2005 and many followed. Richard continues to serve Pakistan today but now remotely and sadly there are still reports of extreme persecution. Last year (2023), Richard was informed of 28 churches being attacked at one time with some of those churches burnt to the ground. Due to the extreme poverty and persecution in the country, it is often the case that pastor's homes also function as their church buildings rendering some families homeless as their churches were destroyed. Those injured were forced to go to hospitals where the quality of care is minimal again due to poverty. The conditions are so bad that even if you met the strict criteria to receive healthcare you may be reluctant to go because of the financial cost and risk of contagion from other illnesses lurking at the hospital.

It is a miracle in itself that some Christians continue to be bold for The Lord despite living in such a country as Pakistan. They have the power of God running through their veins enabling them to do the impossible. At the first meeting Richard spoke at on his first visit to Pakistan, Aiza sold her engagement ring to pay for the food for the pastors attending. She had seen the Kingdom that is not of this world through Jesus and found the ability to see beyond the trials she was facing and the materials of this world. To an even higher degree, this is Rasheed's story who has survived many a lion's den experience.

In Pakistan, the Kingdom of God is prevalent and God's people deeply authentic. People like Rasheed and Aiza are hidden heroes in this world, far greater than the Christian celebrities that may well be genuine but know nothing of the Kingdom of God compared to Christians like this.

What Richard's inbox labelled as 'junk' was actually a golden email from one of the most courageous and faithful Christians in this whole world.

Chapter 20

India

In 2006, The Lord led Richard to India. It would be logical to assume that this door opened through Pakistan as the countries are next door to each other but the connection would initially come from a friend called David back near home. David had a friend named Thankachan whom he had served directly with a number of visits to India himself. Richard and Thankachan had then begun to email through David. To affirm an idea that David and Richard then had of Living Hope Ministries exploring mission opportunities in India, two other gentlemen began to contact Richard from India. Like Rasheed, these two gentlemen had found Richard through the Living Hope Ministries' website and were keen to receive biblical teaching and other support. Confusingly, they had the same surname so it took a while for Richard to realise he was definitely exchanging emails with two people rather than one!

The three enthusiastic Indian contacts and David's experience and invitation were more than enough to persuade Richard to add another stamp to his passport so off he went, accompanied by David.

The temperature, climate and hostility were very similar to Pakistan and at points, India would be seen as even more of a country renowned for persecution of Christians than India but for whatever reason, it is perhaps less publicised and it is certainly a country more known for its colourful garlands. In both Pakistan and India, Richard would need to get used to wearing flowers around his neck to ensure he embraced that alien but harmless element of the cultures!

During the visit, Richard connected well with all three Indians he had contacted previously but in time, The Lord made it clear that the one named S.J. would be his main long-term contact. Once again, this was through similar personalities and visions that highlighted greater hope of fulfilling God's goals for Living Hope Ministries.

India would be another country with a particular hunger for spiritual food. Like other places desperate for hope and healing, thousands would gather at the many crusades and conferences organised.

Seas of faces with individuals easily lost in the crowd made it that despite Richard's servant heart, it was impossible for him to remember each one and assist all. Thankfully, as Richard would travel home feeling a heavy burden for those that he never had time to speak to and pray with, he handed them to The Lord collectively, finding peace that only The Lord could be their Saviour and knowing he (Richard) was only one way of many that The Lord would reach out to them.

Chapter 21

Germany

Tragically, Germany will always be remembered for the Great War and World War 2 but it is perhaps easy to forget that Germany also suffered greatly and like with any country not everyone in the country desired war or violence. For a long time, East Germany was a place of poverty and ruin. In fairly recent times, the West saved the East but like everywhere, spiritual poverty is vast.

Given the brutal treatment of people in Poland at the hands of Germans, it is quite incredible to think that Richard would find a path to Germany through German Christians attending a conference in Poland.

Whilst speaking at a special conference where numerous nationalities were represented in The Name of Jesus, another Andrzej approached Richard. This Andrzej was from Germany and was keen for Richard to come and speak at a weekend conference at his church to encourage and challenge those gathered.

Unusually, the trip to Germany turned out to be a one off and Richard was never invited again. Maybe they decided that they did not like Richard's speaking after all but far more likely, it was probably simply that his input was only needed on that particular occasion. Due to this German church having many more resources than most of the other countries Richard and the rest of Living Hope Ministries serve, this affirms this writer's suspicions.

Chapter 22

Sierra Leone

On 23rd February 2013, Kei Kamara became the first footballer from Sierra Leone to score a goal in Premier League history as his side, Norwich City defeated Everton in an exciting 2-1 victory at Carrow Road!

Despite being his boyhood and forever favourite football team due to his place of birth, this is not Richard's most memorable Sierra Leone related moment.

As much as Kamara's powerful goal left a mark on Richard, going to prison in Sierra Leone would hold a stronger place in his mind.

Thankfully, he went there as a chaplain not a convict but before we enter between those bars, here's how Richard ended up there...

Similarly to how Richard's friendships in Asia came about, a young Christian leader contacted Richard through the Living Hope Ministries website. Emmanuel of Sierra Leone quickly developed a strong rapport with Richard and in 2009, along with his Fakenham friend Chris, Richard ventured to what used to be known as: 'The White Man's Grave'.

Sierra Leone was given this label mainly due to the concerningly high number of malaria-related deaths amongst Europeans living there in the past. It is still one of the most dangerous and deprived areas of Africa but thankfully there have been some improvements in recent times.

Not before long, Richard would be invited to preach to prisoners in one of Sierra Leone's largest jails through Emmanuel's connections.

Richard felt strongly that The Lord wanted him to speak on two particular subjects. One was for those who were in the men's section of the prison and the other for those in the ladies' section.

As Richard stood before the non-standard congregations, Chris sat watching those around with a degree of anxiety. As Richard shared his first message to the men, he spoke boldly about the two criminals who were beside Jesus upon crosses when He hung from His. One of the criminals was at least in time, humbled by Jesus and seemingly repentant of his sin. The other was abusive to Jesus throughout. As Richard delivered the message, Chris wondered how much the convicts around him were likely to be offended and possibly even violently react if they were anything like the second criminal on the cross that Richard mentioned! Similarly, as Richard spoke to the ladies about The Lord Jesus offering forgiveness to a woman caught in adultery, Chris wondered whether these female convicts, some of whom were imprisoned for killing their husbands for committing adultery may also not respond favourably!

By God's grace, in both situations, Richard and Chris were protected and many lives were helped and some even found Jesus through the messages. To this day, it tickles Chris that Richard was so focused on preaching the messages that he felt The Lord gave him, that he was oblivious to the fact they could have been his last had a riot erupted!

Chapter 23

Croatia

As the work in Africa continued to grow with Sierra Leone becoming another key focus for Living Hope Ministries, The Lord simultaneously continued to expand the work of Living Hope Ministries elsewhere, including in Europe.

Working through Zeljko, Living Hope Ministries entered uncharted territory in new and unprecedented ways with an approach that would significantly change the work of the charity in Europe...

As Richard sat in his office, tackling applications for visas for volunteers who had kindly agreed to join him on trips, the phone rang.

'Hi Richard, it's Zeljko. I would like to invite you to be the main speaker at a conference I am organising in my hometown in Croatia. It won't be a Living Hope Ministries event but I would love you to come and represent Living Hope Ministries rather than myself'.

Due to the strength of their friendship, Richard did not take too long praying over this decision and was soon on his way to yet another new country.

The conference was held in a church led by a friend of Zeljko's and Zeljko had invited brothers and sisters in Christ from various parts of Europe. During his time at Bible college in Croatia, he had made connections with believers all across that continent who were also studying there at the time, making it possible for him to invite such a diverse group to the conference.

After this initial trip to Croatia, two Living Hope Ministries' conferences took place there at later dates. Inspired by Zeljko's idea, Richard worked with Zeljko and together they combined their contacts and invited many more friends to these conferences from various churches across Europe. Representatives from Bosnia, Poland, Romania, Serbia and Slovenia all gathered in Jesus' Mighty Name!

This style of conference then progressed with people coming together in a similar manner in Bosnia and Poland making it that no sole country became the 'go to' place or centre in an unhelpful way spiritually or practically.

This new method would continue with and without Richard, making it that Richard was increasingly not needed to connect countries together to build each other up in the Christian faith. It is exciting to highlight that the friendships made through these conferences have gone beyond the conferences which is one of the most beautiful blessings of being in God's immeasurable, worldwide family. People from across the continent continue to support one another because of the work of Living Hope Ministries and others and this inspiring European initiative has gone global as Living Hope Ministries contacts connect with one another due to God working through the charity to bring people together who are not worlds but countries apart.

Chapter 24

Ethiopia

Ethiopia became another country that Living Hope Ministries would play a part in supporting through a brother in Ethiopia reaching out to Richard. Like others, he had come across Living Hope Ministries on the internet and began a friendship with Richard initially through phone calls and emails.

Trips to Ethiopia would once again be very similar to other trips to other African countries whilst having its own unique qualities and challenges. Ethiopia is another one of the particularly poverty stricken parts of Africa and has had a lot of media coverage, not least for all the attention directed there through the famous Band Aid and Live Aid events and songs. It has been calculated that Band Aid and Live Aid combined raised approximately $150 million to help tackle famine in Ethiopia. This sounds like a HUGE figure and of course in one sense it is and definitely was significant but when poverty is so desperate that it is immeasurable, Ethiopia remains a country in great need.

It is challenging going to such environments and when you are on mission, far more than a bus ride from home, it is understandable that you would want to be at least a 'tad early' to the airport.

Richard's Ethiopian contact 'Tadele' would exhibit behaviours that resembled the sound of his name. He was and is one of the most organised brothers in Christ that Richard works with.

Meeting him was a welcome change from meeting yet another brother in Christ who would give him the unpredictable experience of 'African time' rather than time for a coffee at the airport. However, this would not stop a race against time experience for Richard on one Ethiopia trip...

Around 2010, as another successful mission trip came to an end, a weary Richard smiled as he sat with his hand luggage on his lap, chauffeured to the airport in a rusty 4x4. He looked forward to having a sleep on the plane home and then not before long being able to enjoy the comforts of home and of course, seeing Elaine and any of the five boys that may be about. By now three of them had left home so it was not quite the same home it used to be.

Thinking of that well-welcome sleep that he would have, his eyelids started to feel heavy and he drifted off for a nap in the car. He smiled as he saw a sign for the airport as he then went to the land of nod. It read that he was 20 miles away but that was the first airport sign he had seen so was a friendly comfort though they were tight for time.

Not long after that, Richard was suddenly awoken by the sound of screeching tyres and the motion of the 4x4 racing to the left lane and promptly pulling over on the edge of the road.

'Sorry Richard', the driver said.

'There is something wrong with the vehicle'.

Richard was wide awake now and highly concerned about the likely possibility of missing the flight. He waited in the vehicle whilst the driver checked the car over.

'It's a flat tyre Richard'.

Richard felt a degree of relief, knowing it was not the engine or anything else complex.

'I will call brother Tadele and see if he can send someone with a tyre as I do not have a spare'.

Richard's eyebrows raised as he bit his tongue, wanting to ask why they did not have a spare tyre but quickly remembering their poverty and remembering the importance of grace even in challenging times!

Richard just kept quiet and prayed and hoped and waited. After some time of praying, hoping and waiting, another brother in Christ whom Richard had not met before, arrived with another tyre and changed it in lightning speed! He changed it so quickly that Richard wondered if it had been put on right!

He then continued to pray, hope and wait as he wondered whether the plane had been delayed so that he might get home that day as planned and wanted.

He had no phone app or other way of finding out if the plane was delayed so just had to continue praying, hoping and waiting!

The driver was very enthusiastic but that was challenging as though he was in the driving seat of the car, he was not at the steering wheel of the plane!

As they arrived at the airport, Richard leapt out of the car, gave the driver a swift handshake and word of thanks and ran for the plane. He would grab a wing if he had to!

Thankfully, the plane was delayed so Richard did not miss his flight but Elaine still received a particularly long hug when he arrived home that day!

Chapter 25

Serbia

Through the conferences in Croatia, Richard met a gentleman called Tony from Slovenia and a gentleman called Robert from Serbia. You will not be surprised to hear that through these introductions, trips to Slovenia and Serbia soon followed the entrance to Croatia! As you may have noticed, new countries for Living Hope Ministries to serve in, almost always come through a new contact/friend found from those countries.

Unlike many of the Eastern European countries that Living Hope Ministries serve in any way, Serbia is politically connected with Russia. From a worldwide Christian family view, this is of course in one sense irrelevant as we should all love and care for one another regardless of political differences. However, it is of course important for Richard and others to be knowledgeable of political differences and mindful of the sensitivities of such matters as any Christian can get tripped up by politics. The consequences of politics and getting tripped up by politics can both be disastrous after all.

Richard has visited Robert in Serbia on just two occasions but nevertheless these were significant occasions. Richard's main goal was to support Robert pastorally. It has often been the case, especially in more recent years that Richard's focus when visiting other countries is more on delivering pastoral support to individuals to help them lead others rather than preaching at many events. He has always had at least some time in the pulpit (or its equivalent!) on every trip he has been on but his role in leading others has increasingly become more subtle whilst remaining influential.

Serbian churches like many Eastern European churches, do not usually have their own buildings due to poverty but instead use their houses. In this respect, the Serbian trips have been particularly similar to visits to its neighbouring country, Romania.

For a long time Robert was a leader playing a similar role to an elder in a house church consisting of around 12-15 church members. He works for a pharmaceutical company to earn a wage and like all Christians should, sees his workplace as one of his mission fields. Excitingly, he has helped people come to know The Lord Jesus through this particular mission field and God has been at work so mightily that this has led him to plant a church that he holds in his home, primarily for those people.

This is both an encouragement and challenge to us to start or continue being bold and intentional for The Lord in our workplaces.

Robert continues to earn his wage through his pharmaceutical work whilst being a pastor for the church plant in his spare time! His workplace appears to be a vital way of staying connected to the world (in the right sense) so that he can connect them to The Lord and help them stay connected to Him.

Chapter 26

Slovenia

Due to the depressions caused by war and economy crises, Slovenia tragically has high rates of suicide so it is a country particularly in need of visits from messengers of God offering hope. However, that was not the reason for Richard's first and sole visit to Slovenia.

As expressed previously, Richard connected with Tony from Slovenia through one of the conferences in Croatia that Zeljko organised so the door opened the same way as it opened to Serbia. Similarly to the Serbia connection, Richard would mainly serve Slovenia through pastoral support to a key leader rather than through delivering a high quantity of preaching and teaching. Unlike the Serbia connection, The Lord would work through the visit to Slovenia to bless the European country but simultaneously bless beyond that!

As Tony shared with Richard and they prayed together, The Lord shone a light on Rasheed and Pakistan. Tony increasingly felt a heavy heart for them both and sensed he needed to do something to help this dear brother with the countless trials he faced and faces in one of the most challenging parts of Asia.

Tony and his church of around 30 people began stretching out in prayer for Rasheed and Pakistan, interceding for them with their souls laid bare before The Lord desperate to see Him move mightily for them. Though we cannot always see the results of our prayers clearly, my personal belief is that when we pray something that is of The Lord like these Slovenians did, The Holy Spirit always moves in response.

However, one clear reply from The Lord was leading the Slovenians of Tony's church to give Rasheed a generous financial gift to help him with at least some of the trials he was facing at that specific point in time.

Though Tony and Richard remain friends and in contact, Richard never returned to Slovenia because in terms of mission, the Living Hope Ministries' mission was completed through God's powerful work in all of the above.

This is all perhaps a helpful lesson or reminder that The Lord is consistent but not predictable!

Chapter 27

Burundi

The introduction to Burundi was bittersweet. Augustine from Rwanda had a very caring wife called Teddy who had a heavy heart for Burundi. She desired strongly to reach out to the people there but before she had a chance, her life come to an early end as is the case for so many Africans due to extreme poverty. As you may be aware, the life expectancy is much shorter there than those privileged to live outside of the third world. In Rwanda, living 66 years would be considered average and poor Teddy did not even make that. However, we know The Lord knew what He was doing when He took her home at a time that appeared early to those left behind.

Richard and another local pastor in Sussex, England named John, both had a good friendship with Augustine and sensed that The Lord wanted them to fulfil something of Teddy's dream to stretch out to Burundi.

Tragically, Burundi is another African country to have experienced the brutality of genocide and on more than one occasion. It has that horrific resemblance with its neighbouring country Rwanda.

Richard and John ventured to Burundi via Rwanda but the two countries are not happy neighbours, making it particularly challenging crossing the border.

Augustine organised a trustworthy driver to take Richard and John by road from Rwanda to Burundi and Augustine connected them with a brother in Christ called Jeremy. The Lord affirmed Jeremy as being His choice of contact through a group of English Christians from another part of Sussex who were missionaries in South Africa and were able to contact Jeremy more easily than Augustine. As a

Rwandan, the hostility between Burundi and Rwanda did not make it easy for Augustine to make everything as smooth for Richard and John as he wanted, in connecting them to Jeremy. The Lord is so kind in how He makes a way where there is no way and in how He even works out the fine details to protect and bless His people and indeed, His whole creation.

As time went on, Jeremy ended up moving to the USA and the long-term contact for Burundi became a brother called Eddy.

Eddy is another 'Hero of the faith' who has been persecuted for his faith and even wrongly imprisoned. Due to that imprisonment and other walls that for whatever reason, The Lord chose to not knock down, the connection between Living Hope Ministries and Burundi became a technological one after a small number of initial visits.

Living Hope Ministries has played a key role in enabling some of the folk in Burundi to obtain Bibles. Although the charity has done this for other countries, it has not often been on the same scale as this provision to Burundi.

Another significant service from Living Hope Ministries was providing laptops for some of the Burundian leaders. Through these laptops, the leaders are able to develop their ministries, especially in terms of Christian literature and they are also able to attend Living Hope Ministries' meetings online.

Chapter 28

Ecuador

In 2008, Richard and Elaine went on holiday to New Zealand where they visited some friends including Dave and Claire, a couple mentioned earlier in this book.

Richard and Elaine wisely and rightly do not take a holiday from listening to God so it is no surprise that during their visit, they heard The Lord speaking in different ways.

In one church meeting they attended with their friends, a particularly clear word was spoken...

'Richard, I think that The Lord is saying that He is calling you to South America' said a sister in Christ. Her voice was full of confidence and conviction.

And then The Lord chose to be silent on the matter and for a number of years. He planted the seed in Richard and Elaine's hearts and minds at the perfect time and would water it in due course.

About eight years later, the watering can arrived and in the form of another sister in Christ.

This sister lived in England and had kindly donated Christian literature for Living Hope Ministries to pass on to the countries it served on a number of occasions. During one of her conversations with Richard, she mentioned in passing that she had a link in South America. As she said this, it was like Richard went back to that moment in New Zealand where The Lord had highlighted South America. As the conversation continued, it was like a blurry picture becoming clear with Richard realising that Ecuador was the country that The Lord was specifically highlighting at that time and a friend of the sister's called Ramario was the contact to connect with.

After meeting Ramario in Ecuador and serving with him for a season, once again, the long-term contact would not be the initial contact. Through Ramario, Richard was introduced to a man called Antonio. Unlike Ramario, Antonio did not speak English so in the early days Richard had to rely entirely on Ramario and others to translate for Antonio. In time, through developing their friendship, Richard and Antonio would learn to communicate through non-offensive hand gestures and other creative methods but to this day, a translator ensures that the communications are understood correctly. Antonio is one of Richard's closest friends which is such a testimony to how The Holy Spirit enables us to connect spiritually when there are literally 'no words'.

One of the reasons that Antiono is one of Richard's closest friends is due to Richard needing to particularly trust Antonio in some of Richard's most extraordinary adventures and Antonio proving to be trustworthy indeed.

One unique characteristic of Ecuador in comparison to most of the other countries Richard has visited is the incredibly high altitude that literally takes your breath away. The whirling roads that lead you higher and higher up a mountainside to the point that you feel you can touch the clouds are quite an experience. The experience is 'heightened' by the fact that at many points there are no barriers on the side of the roads. If a driver lost concentration or lost control of the vehicle due to a sudden tyre puncture or something else unexpected, you would literally fall off the side of the road into a deep abyss, unlikely to be found quickly and certain to meet our Maker bar an outstanding miracle!

Perhaps the best Ecuador story in the Living Hope Ministries' memory bank is that of Richard and others going deep into a jungle to provide pastoral support and teaching to a tribe that had formerly cut people's heads off, shrunk them down in the horrific process and sold them on the black market! However, the story of their conversion goes before Living Hope Ministries. A friend of Living Hope Ministries had bravely gone into the jungle before Richard had even had the privilege of knowing him, after a powerful call from The Lord where he put himself and his family in seriously grave danger by going to the jungle when they were still shrinking heads and preaching The Gospel! After initially causing the man and his family hardship but thankfully nothing that caused long-term injury, the chief of the tribe fell to his knees and gave his life to The Lord and his people followed. A tribe with so much blood on their hands accepted their need for The Blood of The Lamb and left their rage to pursue The Prince of Peace!

Chapter 29

USA

In 2015, Richard travelled to the States to fellowship with a church in Mississippi. A few years before this, the church in Mississippi had begun a friendship with the church in Lancing, England where Richard has served as an elder and associate pastor for many years now. The organisation known as the 'Fellowship of Independent Evangelical Churches' (FIEC) connected the two churches together initially and it was an obvious and safe avenue to explore.

The church turned out to be another particularly significant connection, mainly through Richard developing a friendship with a brother called Jose further, who most helpfully became a much needed translator and co-missioner for Richard's visits to Ecuador and interactions with Ecuador and Peru via internet communications. A lady called Maria Jose has also given priceless support in some of these areas of work.

However, 2015 was not the first time Richard had visited the United States of America!

Prior to the trip to Mississippi, Richard had visited New Jersey, Chicago and Minnesota.

The visit to Minnesota is memorable partly because it took place just after the I-35W bridge tragically collapsed in 2007. The wife of the person that Richard was visiting had driven over the bridge not long before it collapsed! We are grateful to The Lord for sparing her but our hearts continue to go out to those who lost loved ones due to that terrible incident.

The person Richard visited for that trip was the brother of Rasheed from Pakistan who had been blessed with an opportunity to move there, away from the fierce persecution of his home country. Richard felt that it was important to go there to encourage him because although life was far easier there than in Pakistan, USA still has its challenges especially for those alien to the 'USA way'. Whilst there, Richard was also able to preach on a handful of occasions.

Winding the clock back 20 years before the Minnesota experience, the visit to Chicago took place. A Nigerian brother who lived in Chicago invited Richard over to Chicago but never showed up at the airport! The Lord took hold of the trip and used other contacts to enable Richard to preach in a number of settings.

Any anxieties the 'No-show' at the airport brought Richard were quickly lessened by the gun shot sounds he heard and a brother gently informing him not to worry as

'...we often have people shot around here!'

Thankfully, by God's grace, Richard, absolutely incredibly, never on that trip or on any trip to this day, has had even one hair touched on his head!

Richard's first trip to America was perhaps the most significant. In 1995, a Kenyan brother strongly advised Richard to go to New Jersey where the brother had contacts and to use the visit as an opportunity to try and gain sponsors for Living Hope Ministries. The churches Richard ended up visiting did not have the means to support Richard but he benefited from the experience of preaching at one of the churches and he received a very special message from The Lord himself from another speaker in one setting where Richard just sat quietly and unknown in the congregation...

The speaker approached Richard as he sat with his head bowed. He had paused his preaching as he felt led to prophesy over people. Richard was one of those people. Laying his hand on Richard's shoulder he declared to him:

'Bible teacher!'

He walked away but soon returned to Richard...

'You have been working in the dark and not many knew what was happening in your life but God knew! Brother, God knew! God was raising you up! Your ministry is going to take off and take off and take off! I see you preaching! I see you giving out books! Bible teacher!'

I think you have seen enough already to see that this prophecy came true but there is still more to tell. Next stop, North Macedonia!

Chapter 30

North Macedonia

The friendship between Richard and Zeljko has been a key factor for the work of Living Hope Ministries broadening increasingly over the years in Europe along with Richard's friendship with Andrzej from Poland.

North Macedonia was a trip very much initiated by Zeljko introducing Richard to his friends Svetla and Luckie.

They are a couple who lead a church of around 30 people in a small building.

Although Richard has only visited North Macedonia on one occasion, his time there was once again significant as was his fellowship with Svetla and Luckie there and when seeing them at a number of the European conferences.

Unusually for a couple leading a ministry, Svetla and Luckie are both pretty much as involved as each other sharing the workload of looking after their church very evenly.

One of their main challenges is living somewhere where there are many beautiful, eye-catching   church buildings surrounded at times by wonderful scenery including some impressive lakes.

This is a challenge because churches there are very much seen and used as a key part of North Macedonia's tourism like in other places such as Italy. Although this regular access and exposure of churches could potentially be seen as a way of creating evangelistic opportunities, it can also be a way of people struggling to see churches as anything other than tourist attractions.

Svetla and Luckie want to see heaven come to earth through the fruits of The Spirit being evident in North Macedonia rather than a heavenly looking location that misses the King of Heaven and Lord of All from its focus.

Richard's time in North Macedonia played another important part in him understanding the diverse cultures and backgrounds of Europeans. Time and time again, he has seen the value in 'knowing your audience' so that you can serve them better: a good lesson or reminder for us all.

Chapter 31

Bulgaria

Interestingly, Svetla of North Macedonia was born in Bulgaria. You could see how The Lord could well have used that background to open a door into Bulgaria for Living Hope Ministries. However, as already expressed, The Lord is not predictable and Svetla did not turn out to be The Lord's way of sending Living Hope Ministries to Bulgaria...

An inspirational couple in England named Nigel and Val serve The Lord in all sorts of bold and exciting ways including through prison ministry in Sussex. They have many Christian friends around the world whom they support through prayer and other means. One of those friends is a man named Pepe who lives in Bulgaria. They connected their friend Richard with their friend Pepe and Richard visited Pepe to encourage him and spur him on with the great work that he was and is doing out there. Like with North Macedonia, Richard would only visit Bulgaria once and like with North Macedonia there is therefore not too much to tell about Richard's experience there. However, the story of Pepe is particularly worth a read and after reading it, you'll understand why a pastoral visit from Richard to help Pepe keep fighting the good fight of faith made Bulgaria yet another significant connection for Living Hope Ministries...

'Pepe, we need you to come immediately' Aleksandar said urgently as soon as Pepe answered his phone.

'Pastor Rayko has died'.

Pepe sat down with his phone hanging loosely in his hand by his side and his other hand on his head.

'Pepe, can you come?' Aleksandar pressed.

'Sorry Aleksandar. Yes of course. I will be there in 15 minutes. Let me

just explain to my manager'.

Pepe was a well-respected member of his church and had been called upon in crisis situations before but this was on another level! Thankfully, few people have to help their church deal with the death of their pastor. Pepe looked at his oboe that he had been practising prior to the call and placed it in its case and picked up his phone again and searched his contacts for 'Ivan' and hit the call button.

He took a deep breath and waited for Ivan to take the call which Ivan quickly did.

'Ivan, I am so sorry for the short notice but I am not going to be able to accompany the orchestra on the tour. I have just found out that my pastor has died and I need to be there to help the church'.

Ivan was happy to support Pepe and find someone to stand in. Pepe was committed to his work with the orchestra and Ivan knew it would take a real exception for him to have to pull out of a tour.

After helping the church through their initial grieving process, the congregation increasingly looked to him for leadership, guidance and pastoral support.

As the years have gone by, his hours with the orchestra have reduced as he has naturally and supernaturally fulfilled the role of pastor in his church.

He never sought this role but God clearly planned it and The Lord has blessed him so much in the role that he now oversees 3 churches in Bulgaria!

You can now see why along this journey, a visit from someone with the unique role of being 'a pastor for pastors' was priceless for Pepe.

The Lord knows what we need and will send us help from down the road, around the corner, a few countries away and even across the world.

He did this for Pepe, He has done this for others mentioned and not mentioned in this book and He has done this for Richard.

The Lord knows the right people to send to us to encourage us and to help us achieve His perfect purposes. He also knows the right times to send them, even if it does not seem quick enough to us due to our inferior understanding.

Chapter 32

The Democratic Republic of the Congo

You may be aware that there are two countries in Africa with the name 'Congo'. The two countries are neighbours in central Africa.

One is named 'The Republic of the Congo' and the other: 'The Democratic Republic of the Congo'. Richard has never been to the first but has been to the latter and here's how he gained a connection to the DRC...

'Pastor Richard' called a nearby voice soon after a mud hut meeting in Kenya had taken place where Richard had been speaking.

Richard stepped forward and gladly received a handshake from the gentleman who had drawn his attention.

'I am Pastor Isaac from the Congo'.

Richard was amazed. He knew it was no small feat that this brother had journeyed all this way to be at the meeting. What Richard did not know but later found out was that Isaac had made an EPIC journey to be there and that it was not the first or last time he would do so, joining with brothers in Kenya and at other times, Uganda.

To get from the DRC to Kenya or Uganda would sometimes require Isaac to have to ride on the back of a motorbike, to then sail on a boat where on departure he would find a bus to travel on before finally hiring a bicycle for the last stretch! If ever there was a powerful message to help us overcome any obstacles that may cause us to miss church regularly, this testimony would probably be it!

For that testimony and others, Isaac is another notable 'hero of the faith!'

Not long after meeting Isaac, Richard was invited to the DRC where he took a much easier but still unusual journey there himself. To get deep into the DRC by plane, Richard flew in a Mission Aviation Fellowship plane from Uganda. MAF planes are petite planes designed to take emergency and mission workers into remote areas where larger aircraft would be unable to land safely and where airlines would have little interest from paying customers. Going to destinations like this comes with high risks and no option of a comfortable hotel.

The roads in the DRC have for many years been intentionally neglected, leading to rough travelling. This is another reason for unusual methods being used to travel to and from the country. Keeping the roads from being anything but pristine has been one method to try and keep outsiders from coming in and stealing the precious stones and gold that the DRC is famous for.

Before flying the plane, the pilot unlike any other pilot Richard had met before, prayed before his advance on the runway. Prayer is a key value and action of MAF and of Living Hope Ministries and with the many dangers of places like the DRC, it would be particularly unwise not to pray fervently.

Richard's main memory of his time in the DRC is not of conferences or meetings, as important as they were but of another memorable car journey. Richard experienced another punctured tyre episode like he had in Ethiopia but unlike in Ethiopia the concern was not on getting home that day but rather whether he would get home at all!

Soon after happening to travel between two United Nations' trucks armed with unnerving machine gun units, the trucks went elsewhere and the vehicle Richard was travelling in submitted to the neglected roads with the puncture mentioned above.

The area where the vehicle had submitted lay in what was known as the 'Red Zone'. This zone was an area that terrorists had regularly targeted passengers in vehicles travelling through.

Aware of the danger they, especially the 'rich-looking white man' were in, Isaac acted quickly and arranged for a friend to come and pick them up on his moped where Isaac, Richard and his belongings were taken to a safe place. Those left with the puncture were thankfully also protected from any harm.

Isaac, like Richard but to an even greater level has survived many a danger but tragically not every danger. Not so long ago, Issac was poisoned and it was quite possibly by wolves in sheep's clothing due to jealousy of his admirable walk with The Lord Almighty. Issac never recovered from the attack and is sadly no longer with us on this earthly journey but like all true followers of The Lord, he is sleeping and will be seen again!

His son, Daniel has picked up his legacy. In fairly recent times, he was also poisoned by opposition! Thankfully, he lives to tell the tale himself and continues to hold 'The Name that saves' high!

Chapter 33

Finland

Similarly to some of the other trips mentioned in this book, Finland was primarily a pastoral visit rather than one with a prime focus on preaching and teaching like the majority of Richard's trips have been.

You may remember a gentleman named 'Bishop Stephen' highlighted in an earlier chapter as being a particularly dear friend of Richard's. Richard always felt like part of the family when he visited Stephen before he went home to The Lord. This was because Stephen's whole family would treat him as such including Stephen's daughter Naomi.

A little while after losing her earthly father, Naomi went to live in Finland where she studied and met a man who would later become her husband. Out of a kind of duty of care from having such a strong relationship with Stephen and warm welcome from Stephen's family, Richard felt it was right to go and visit Naomi and her husband in Finland. As hoped, the pastoral visit had a highly positive impact on both Naomi and her husband along with a small group that the couple attended where Richard shared about some of the wonderful work The Lord was doing through Living Hope Ministries.

There have been other occasions in the UK and beyond where Richard has felt it was right to pay similar visits.

Another particularly notable occasion was when Richard went to support Bitrus' wife, Betty in Nigeria after Bitrus sadly left this earth due to severe illness. Betty picked up the mantle fairly instantly after losing her husband to ensure the work he had begun carried on and prospered. Betty appears to be a Deborah of our time!

Chapter 34

Colombia

One of the main purposes that The Lord seems to have had for and with Living Hope Ministries is to help Christians to have a 'World Vision'. To be more specific, this means helping Christians to think outside of their families, churches, communities and even countries. With wars, natural disasters, famines and all sorts of atrocities (some even unspeakable because they are so evil) happening in the world, it is particularly important for Christians to pray for others beyond their borders and to take action in other ways when The Lord leads.

Over the years, Richard has increasingly encouraged those he interacts with, especially leaders due to their influence on others, to have this world vision.

In addition to encouraging this with words, where he has sensed it is right, Richard has also stood with brothers and sisters in taking this bold step. In practice, this regularly comes in the form of organising prayer meetings to intercede for the nations but it has at times also meant journeying with someone to a country that they feel a burden for. The mission to Colombia arose from such circumstances as these.

After asking Antonio of Ecuador to consider reaching out to another country, Antonio prayerfully decided that Colombia was in The Lord's plans for him and others.

Richard and Jose accompanied Antonio for the first trip there and it was eventful to say the least!

Antonio made contact with a brother called Fabian who along with his wife, was very busy serving The Lord through leading a church and taking Christian support to a local prison. As indicated elsewhere in this book, prison ministry has been another important element of

Living Hope Ministries.

Richard has preached at a number of prisons across the world and offered pastoral support to prisoners. Among other instances, Richard has preached over the phone to prisoners in Ethiopia, physically visited prisoners in Malawi and the USA and played a part in Nigel and Val's prison work in the UK at times.

The prison ministry in Colombia is perhaps the most spectacular among all of these immensely important and fruitful prison ministries that Richard has been involved in.

Fabian, his wife and the rest of their prison ministry team invest an exceptionally high amount of time and prayer into that area of ministry and have seen incredible changes in people's lives as a result of God's grace responding to those efforts.

Not only have they led people to The Lord through the ministry and carried out discipleship programmes in and out of the jail for prisoners but they have even actively sought out potential pastors through the work!

As you can imagine, the impact of investing in prisoners to such a high level brings immeasurable hope for the prisoners and communities witnessing such change in the prisoners. It also enables people to become pastors who can relate to those entrapped in darkness in a way that pastors from a smoother background never could!

By God's grace, Richard has always made it out of prison but on the prison visit in Colombia it looked a little bit uncertain for a moment when they vigorously checked his fingerprints on his departure to check they were definitely the same fingerprints as the man who imprinted them on entry!

It was indeed Richard on both occasions but presumably his fingerprints coming out looked slightly different so required extra attention.

Chapter 35

Commissioning the Missioning

Before the worldwide debilitating covid storm hit the UK in 2020, The Lord had graciously prepared Living Hope Ministries for such a pandemic!

In the early years of the charity, the main work of Living Hope Ministries was travelling abroad as often as possible and across the UK to share testimonies of what The Lord was doing abroad and to gain support. Hence why that has been the main emphasis of this book. However, as the years have gone by whilst still having the above as a main focus, remote methods of working have increasingly developed especially in terms of Living Hope Ministries' radio programmes and television programmes that air in multiple countries and via various forms of social media.

The creation and development of live Mobile Phone Conferences has also been a notable ministry for the charity. By 2019, Living Hope Ministries' teachings were being shared almost every day of the week through these Mobile Phone Conferences. Regular Mobile Phone Conferences, where Richard and others deliver teaching to groups over the phone with a recipient in another country holding their phone up to a microphone, have increasingly been a Living Hope Ministries' method in a number of countries.

Most of the countries receiving teaching in this way are African and it has always been a useful way of delivering the Word more regularly but it became an inevitable approach when the pandemic prevented people from travelling abroad.

If it was not for The Lord already making the media side of the charity a sizeable element of the work and the Mobile Phone Conferences a regular fixture prior to the pandemic, Living Hope

Ministries could have become a thing of the past when it hit. Instead, remarkably, The Lord had made it ahead of its time in a way that only He could have and with knowledge beyond human understanding!

It is worth noting that in recent times, Richard has begun leading an international Bible School online, highlighting how Living Hope Ministries' approach has expanded over the years. However, now that the pandemic has passed, mission trips have returned to being the main focus of the work but without Richard regularly stepping foot outside of the UK himself anymore.

The pandemic was the cause of Richard's feet having to be grounded at home but since the pandemic, Richard has almost entirely stopped travelling abroad due to recognising that the work will not outlive him if he is the main missioner. After around 25 years of travelling himself, exploring about 25 different countries on mission for Living Hope Ministries, Richard has generally turned his attention to sending others out on mission rather than leaving his home country himself. As Living Hope Ministries reaches its 30th birthday this year, it is true to say that Living Hope Ministries has indeed been around the world in 30 years!

In addition to the countries that he has visited across the years on mission for Living Hope Ministries, Richard has visited a handful of other countries for other purposes. His trip to Israel in 2017 is a particularly significant memory where he had the privilege to see the places where The Lord Jesus walked. This impacted his understanding of Jesus' life greatly and in turn impacted the depth and quality of his preaching.

Although Richard has not stepped into unventured territory for quite some time, some of those that he has met in his lifetime so far have taken that step leading to countries such as Peru, Liberia, Nepal and the Philippines being visited on behalf of Living Hope Ministries by others. As already indicated, Richard has also increasingly stepped back from trips to familiar countries and focused on commissioning and supporting others to do so in his place under the Living Hope Ministries' banner. Brothers and sisters from across the globe now support and/or deliver (and in some cases oversee) the work of Living Hope Ministries in a vast number of countries without any in-person accompaniment from Richard...

Africa

Malawi and Mozambique: Aubrey, Patrick, Almando, Dave and Claire

Zimbabwe: Silas and Scott

Nigeria: Emmanuel

Ghana: Neindo

Sierra Leone: Emmanuel

The Gambia: Jeremiah

Liberia: Samuella

Guinea: Michael

Kenya: Peter M., Silas and Chris

Uganda: Peter K., Roy and Scott

Tanzania: William, David and Jane

Rwanda: Augustine, Emmanuel, Jenny and Alison

Burundi: Eddy, Balthazzar, Aniset, Thierry and Habina

Ethiopia: Tadele

South Sudan: Emmanuel

Congo: Daniel

Europe

Poland: Andrzej

Bosnia: Zeljko, Tea and Christopher

Serbia: Robert

Macedonia: Svetla, Val and Nigel

Romania: Fivi, Terry and Di

Bulgaria:: Pepe and Simon

Ukraine: Andrew and Mike

Finland: Naomi

Spain: Paul and Christine

Asia

India: Bhutan and SJ

Pakistan: Rasheed and David

Philippines: Johny, Dave and Claire

Nepal: Dhan and Wikka

New Zealand: Dave and Claire, John and Delyse

The Americas

Colombia: Fabian

Ecuador: Antonio, Héctor, Jose and Chio

Peru: Luis and Chio

USA: Steve and Jose

Forgive me if your name should have been mentioned in one or more of the continent lists and is not. Please blame that on this author's humanity rather than viewing it as a lack of gratitude or care.

As I mentioned in the introduction of this book, those who have been commissioned and supported by Living Hope Ministries all have their own stories to tell so this book is in one sense a drop in the vast ocean of what The Lord has been doing through Living Hope Ministries. In fact, as you would probably guess, Richard himself and all those connected with Living Hope Ministries in any way at all have far more stories to tell than covered in this book.

'Around the World in 30 Years' is a glimpse of what The Lord has done through Living Hope Ministries so far because no book could be long enough to contain everything and Living Hope Ministries is just one of countless ways that The Lord reaches out to His world every second, every day.

If you truly know The Lord Jesus then you know that *'faith without works is dead'* and that every follower of Jesus is called to mission. It may be to another country (or countries), it will be to the country you live in, it will be to your workplace if you are able to work, it will be to family and friends, the person at the end of the phone when you are sorting out your car insurance and everyone else you will encounter in your life.

Let us daily ask for The Lord's guidance on how to be His hands and feet in any and every situation, discerning when to tell of Him, always aiming to reflect His infallible qualities, willing to go wherever He would lead us and listening to His voice so that we do not miss His direction.

As the hymn proclaims that Richard and Elaine sung wholeheartedly and conscientiously on their wedding day:

'Not a shadow can rise, not a cloud in the skies, but His smile quickly drives it away; not a doubt or a fear, not a sigh or a tear, can abide while we trust and obey!'

Living Hope Ministries' and Author's Contact Information

If you would like to know more about The Lord Jesus or Living Hope Ministries, please feel free to contact us…

Living Hope Ministries' Contact Information:

Richard Brunton: lhm@livinghopeministries.uk

Check out www.livinghopeministries.uk and Living Hope Ministries can also be found on social media.

Author's Contact Information:

Stephen Mark Brunton: fedministries@outlook.com

You can also contact Stephen/Steve on social media through searching for 'FED Ministries' or 'Bible in 12 years' where you will find his Monday-Friday series #Biblein12years available for free.

Other Titles by the Author

All Ten of these Books Below are Purchasable on
www.amazon.com and www.amazon.co.uk

Stephen Mark Brunton's '*Down to Earth*' Book Trilogy:

Volume One- 'Jesus Loves to Drive out Fear'

Volume Two- 'Facing the Reality of Hell (A Call for All Christians to Evangelise)'

Volume Three- 'Prayer is Action'

Stand Alone Titles by Stephen:

'Is God Angry with me?'

'Should the Church Permit Baptism to a Practising Homosexual?'

'Down to Earth with the Street Community'

'Down to Earth Worship Leading'

Stephen's Christian Fictional Piece:

'Tales of the King and Kingdom'

Stephen's Discussion Workbooks:

The 'Down to Earth' Course Handbook

66 Deeper 'Down to Earth' Discussions

Credits

Written by Stephen Mark Brunton.

Front and back covers designed by Charlene Brunton.

The majority of the information provided for this book naturally came from Stephen's online meetings with Richard and Elaine Brunton and Stephen's own experience of Living Hope Ministries and its missions.

All contents proof read by Stephen, Elaine and Richard Brunton.

'Around the World in 30 Years' was published by Verité CM Ltd in Autumn 2024.